SUDDENLY SINGLE

BY
CASH MATTHEWS

Published by:

A Book's Mind

PO Box 272847

Fort Collins, CO 80527

"My mother divorced my father, twice. Then she died. I was helpless.
If this book helps just one person take the right actions,
I will feel like I was a good son."

Cash Matthews

This book is dedicated to moms everywhere. You are grape jelly, and us kids are just crusty loaves of bread.

Before you do anything else,
Read Chapter 4, page 14
Regarding Passwords.

FINANCIAL DISCLAIMER:

In certain parts of this book, we illustrate certain investment rates of return that are NOT guaranteed or estimated. These interest rates are hypothetical and subject to being completely wrong. You must carefully examine the investments you use and determine their efficacy in achieving your results. No particular investments are mentioned in this book. PLEASE DO NOT USE THESE NUMBERS TO CREATE YOUR PLAN unless you have carefully studied the investment markets. No guarantees or outcomes are predicted or suggested in this book. Past investment performance does not predict future results.

Investment advisory services offered through Wealth Watch Advisors, an SEC registered investment advisor. Wealth Watch Advisors and The Solomon Group are independent of one another. Please note, registration with the SEC does not denote a specific skill level or guarantee the success of a particular investment strategy.

TABLE OF CONTENTS

1
NOW WHAT? (PART 1)

"Some people believe holding on and hanging in there are signs of great strength. However, there are times when it takes much more strength to know when to let go, and then do it." – Ann Landers.

I've always admired the wisdom of Ann Landers. She always knows what to do in a tough situation. Perhaps you are feeling a little lost right now, as if the whole world conspired against you and there's nowhere left to run. You may be in a challenging situation where you ask yourself, *"Can I go on?"*

Suddenly, being single is an unexpected and difficult place to be. It is a season filled with unknowns and challenges. Death and divorce can strike suddenly, and the impact can last a lifetime. As much as I would love to provide immediate consolation, writings like this are simply your starting point for recovery. Becoming "Suddenly Single" can be a life changing event, and as painful as it can be, wherever you are, right now, you do not have to stay there.

I'm glad you are reading. Sometimes, having something to pour into can begin to make a difference. There **is** life after tragedy. There **is** hope for those who fight to live another day. In the storm, it can be difficult to get our bearing, and know which direction to go. This book is a step for you. Be proud that you are taking action.

I am a believer that "Action Cures Everything"….A.C.E. During this time, you can be an ACE just by taking each small step in front of you.

Divorce is common for American couples and death is a certainty which no one can escape. Approximately fifty percent of all marriages end up in divorce.[1] The other half ends up in death eventually. Those are grim statistics for sure.

There's a likelihood that either you or your spouse will end up alone at some point. This makes any conversation surrounding this topic essential.

The issues that come with being Suddenly Single are inevitable. Divorce and death of a loved one are quite different, but both have a similar impact on how we perceive and live out our lives - they both create a void and a certain type of loss. You may suffer an economic loss, uncertainty, a changed environment, or fear of the unknown if you have become Suddenly Single. As you know by now, it is a challenging process.

No one needs to be reminded of the statistics when they are now a statistic. Someone else's misery doesn't lessen yours. Misery **doesn't** love company. At this moment, your situation has changed, through no fault or choice of your own. Death or divorce has left you Suddenly Single.

There is no easy way to have these conversations. It is difficult to discuss such a sensitive topic. If I could, I would reach out of this book, give you a hug, and let you know everything will be alright. I've been through this with hundreds of families during my career. They don't talk much about this phenomenon at financial advisor training school, but at this moment, you are facing a mountain. This book will help you climb that mountain. Once you restore your life to your new normal, we can hug then. But for now, let's navigate from where you are to where you want to be. This book can be used as a GPS of sorts: what is the destination?

As the "go-to" financial guy for many families, I've seen what you are seeing from the outside. I've been close to the fire, and I know your journey to create some sort of "new normal" is possible. Again, nothing in this writing will lessen your pain. Nothing here can remove the grief. The point of this book is to let you know there is help available. There are lots of life rafts for you to cling to during a time such as this. When you are ready, you can begin to restore your life. You'll have the tools and hope you need so you can rebuild your life on purpose. I know that recovery isn't the easiest thing to do, but it's often just one straightforward step at a time. In your hands, you are holding one of those steps.

You will hear many comments from well-meaning friends. And your friends **will** have your back for a while. But in time, they will continue living their life. Over the long term, those sentiments will fade, and what remains will be the life **you** rebuild for yourself. Good friends are vital for recovery, restoration, and victory in life. And if you're not ready right now, don't sweat it. It's okay.

Here is an important thing I have learned in the world of recovery: it is easy to fall into the trap of speaking of your situation as part of your identity. Whatever your situation, this is NOT who you are. Obviously, this is important and an "interesting" time. And for a time, you certainly MUST verbalize to friends and family what you are feeling. Honestly, they do care, so let them know what you are going through. And while no science tells you how long to grieve, it's equally important to realize no science tells us when to move forward in our lives.

You will know. Early on, it may seem like it will NEVER get better. But it will get better. You will thrive again, and you can prosper if you work towards it. Right now, it is ok to curl up in the fetal position and lean on your friends and family. It's ok to let them know what you are feeling. This season will evolve for you and each day you can turn another corner.

From a Biblical standpoint, I have always found the Book of Ecclesiastes an interesting read. In this small book, we come to understand the frailty of life, and the concept of passage through time. One of my favorite lines comes in verse 3:3, "a time to tear down and a time to build." Perhaps you are suddenly in the "build mode." Listen to these words:

"There is a time for everything,
and a season for every activity under the heavens:
a time to be born and a time to die,
a time to plant and a time to uproot,
a time to kill and a time to heal,
a time to tear down and a time to build,
a time to weep and a time to laugh,

a time to mourn and a time to dance,

a time to scatter stones and a time to gather them,

a time to embrace and a time to refrain from embracing,

a time to search and a time to give up,

a time to keep and a time to throw away,

a time to tear and a time to mend,

a time to be silent and a time to speak,

a time to love and a time to hate,

a time for war and a time for peace."

GETTING STARTED

Do these verses resonate with you? I believe God saw our situation long in advance, and He gave us words of comfort. This recognition will serve you well as you take the next steps. If this is your time to take the next steps, I have one **strong** recommendation:

GET A SPIRAL NOTEBOOK!

I am a big fan of the 79-cent spiral notebook. I use these for many reasons, but with all of the information coming your way in the coming days, you will need a convenient place to write things down.

Later in this book, we discuss keeping a journal. This is not your journal. This is your playbook. This is your password list. This is your phone number database, as well as your checklist. When you look on the sidelines of an NFL Football game, you always see the coaches and assistant coaches looking in some type of book. The spiral is your recovery and playbook. You will thank me later!!

With the loss of a significant other, either from death or divorce, you're left with these emotions and wondering, '*now what do I do*?' These are normal emotions and normal questions to ask. However, there is life after loss. Soon you will regain control. Getting started can be difficult but staying the same is also difficult. ***Let's get started.***

[1] https://www.wf-lawyers.com/divorce-statistics-and-facts/

[2] https://www.everydayhealth.com/emotional-health/life-after-divorce-12-ways rebuild-your-life/

[1] Ecclesiastes 3 - A Time for Everything (NIV)

2
YOU ARE NOT ALONE!

"I am not alone even in solitude." – Debasish Mridha

I f you are lost or frightened, here is the truth: **you are not alone.** Someone out there is going through the same thing that you are going through right this minute. Knowing these facts doesn't help in the current moment, but it's nice to know we aren't going through something completely alone.

THE RATE OF DIVORCE:

Almost 41% of all first marriages end up in divorce. For subsequent marriages, the likelihood for failure is much higher. In the US, 60 percent of second marriages end up in divorce. For third marriages, 78% fail.[1] To put into perspective how often a divorce happens, I invite you to look at this - by the time a couple finishes reciting their vows (two minutes), almost nine divorces are happening elsewhere in the US.

There are many reasons subsequent marriages fail, but it all points out the complexities of blended families. Everyone has baggage, and there's a chance that you and your spouse will carry out unhealthy relationship patterns that you developed with your previous relationships. Either way, marriage can be complicated, and what once was a lifetime vow has eroded into a statistic that affects millions.

Aside from the high divorce rate in the country, we also boast one of the lowest **married life expectancies,** the time couples stay married. On average, the typical American marriage ending in divorce lasts just eight years. This figure varies by country and by state. Italy has a similar divorce rate to the US, but the average married life expectancy is 17 years. This could mean that the Italians have a higher tolerance level compared to the average American family.

Divorce rates vary just as much by the state in the United States. There are fourteen states with divorce rates of 50-65%. Oklahoma leads that figure with almost 60% of all marriages ending in divorce. A further twelve states have a divorce rate that varies between 15% and 39%, the remaining states falling somewhere in the middle. Hawaii has the highest percentage of married people out of all fifty states - with only 20% of marriages ending in divorce.[3]

THE DEMOGRAPHICS

On average, people who end up filing for their first divorce are around the age of thirty. Divorces are most common among those between 25 and 39, and women are more likely to file for divorce than men.[4]

THE CAUSES OF DIVORCE

At this moment, who really cares what the cause is? You may be in a situation that has multiple causes, and what you seek is a refuge from the storm. I've seen so many different causes of divorce, labeling them here wouldn't add much to a good conversation. I can tell you that most of the divorces I've seen had one problem in common: money issues. While it is socially unacceptable to talk about money (and other things) in public, you and I are brave and strong, so it will be fine to have a conversation about money!

We aren't here to point fingers, but we can learn a great deal from those who have suffered from money woes. Of course, there are MANY other mitigating factors in every divorce, but a brief conversation about money issues may be in order, regardless of your current marital status.

Financial Issues. Money will always be a part of the conversation in any marriage. More than a third of married people mentioned that excessive debt is an enormous factor in the outcome of their marriage. The pressure of messy finances can be a deal breaker. Most families aren't fully educated on money issues, yet it's a common element of everyday life.

As our world becomes more complex, so do the money related problems. With debt plaguing most American households, dual and triple income families are on the rise. With job insecurity, pandemics, and a burdensome tax system, the problems in the world of finance don't seem to be going away any time soon. As you begin your new life, make sure you have a proper command of these money items.

There are many great ideas on money behaviors, and those will be discussed in a later chapter. For now, know that you need to eliminate debt, plan for retirement, and make sure you have enough money to live your daily life. Here are a few things we will address in a later chapter:

- Planning and starting conversations on household budgets.
- Creating a plan for eliminating "bad" household debts.
- Creating a goal plan that is believable and practical.
- Putting financial protection in place, as well as pertinent legal documents, such as your basic will. (See a qualified legal expert for advice on these issues)
- Talking about long-term financial goals, such as retirement or a new home.
- Career and employment development
- Education planning for children or grandchildren.

"Getting Old Ain't for Sissies"
-Geraldine Hart
(My red headed, cigarette smoking, Dr. Pepper addicted Grandmother)

WHY THIS IS IMPORTANT

THE RISK OF POVERTY

About 75% of all women die single. This is especially worrisome considering that women live longer than men. The average age a woman becomes widowed is fifty-seven. This figure does not include women who lost their partners for whom they are not legally married. For men, the figure is a bit conservative. For every four widows, there is only one widower. But this does not mean that dealing with it is easier for men than for women.[6]

For most couples, the risks of going into poverty increase as they become older. The ability to recover from a financial setback later in life is often met with resistance as the income earning capacity during retirement years is usually less. This is especially true for women who are more vulnerable to financial mishaps. This risk is further magnified in the event the woman's spouse dies. The rate of poverty for women aged sixty-five and older is roughly 12%. But for widowed women within the same age group, this risk increases by over four-fold, with over 51% living on less than $22k a year.[7]

YOUNGER WIDOWS AND WIDOWERS

For those widowed at a younger age with children that haven't reached the age of eighteen, the Social Security benefits may kick in to provide some sort of economic assurance for the survivors. This can be paid out to certain family members, including the widows/widower, young children, and dependent parents. While Social Security is traditionally a retirement program, it's also been used as a type of benefit plan to benefit dependent children in the event they lose a parent.

WIDOWS AND WIDOWERS AGED 60 AND BEYOND

Widows/widowers who became widowed past age 60 are usually more vulnerable to a precarious financial situation if they don't have substantial life savings, a guaranteed lifetime income source, pensions, retirement plans, or life insurance. In some cases, the ability to create a new earnings plan is more limited as we age.

WHAT ABOUT SOCIAL SECURITY INCOME?

For a standard couple who are both on Social Security, the loss of a spouse also means a loss of the lower Social Security Amount. When there is a death, your expenses decline, but it is different for every family. After death, you will now only receive the LARGER of the two Social Security Benefits. This is problematic for creating and maintaining your monthly income stream and must be accounted for. Projections indicate for the widowed to maintain the same standard of living as before, they may need a hundred percent of their former income. This can eventually end up in the spiral to poverty. Planning for life post-death is vital given the complexity of today's financial markets.

THE PROBLEM WITH LONGEVITY

Honestly, it really sounds crazy to discuss a long life as a problem. Understand I'm a math nerd, and my brain gravitates to solutions for math problems. We've all prayed for a long, wonderful life, but we also want to have confidence in how to best meet those continued expenses. And once you have created your own success plan, there's one less thing to worry about!

With improvements in the medical field, people today live longer than ever before. To date, men on average are expected to live for 76 years, while women outlive men for at least 5 years. It may sound like a good thing, and it is - but a long life can create even more money concerns. As we age, there is a greater need for medical care, assisted living, home care, and help in our daily lives with homes, cars, and daily activities. My grandmother, Geraldine, used to say, "Getting old ain't for sissies." She was right!

It is not uncommon to see women live over fifteen years as widows. Often, the remaining spouse has a desire to travel, see family, and pursue those things that bring them joy. This may lead to the need for more retirement income to maintain a desired standard of living. How you prepare right now will determine the outcome of how those dreams come to life sometime later.

Let me remind you that you are not alone. You may think that you're all by yourself on this journey, but you're not. While death and divorce are quite different things, planning for and recovering from either share many similarities. Both take action, perseverance, and consistency in financial behavior.

You bought this book…you are reading this book and taking notes…you are beginning to see that the show must go on, and that you are up to the task. These feelings are wonderful and empowering. Taking steps, taking action… these things make you an ACE! Action Cures Everything. Not perfect action, just action.

[1] https://www.wf-lawyers.com/divorce-statistics-and-facts/

[2] Bethink.com

[3] Centers for Disease Control and Prevention. "Marriages and Divorces." [4] Wilkinson & Finkbeiner Family Law. "Divorce Statistics: Over 115 Studies, Facts and Rates for 2018."

[5] Institute for Divorce Financial Analysts. "Survey: Certified Divorce Financial Analyst® (CDFA®) professionals Reveal the Leading Causes of Divorce."

[6] https://www.bedelfinancial.com/75-of-women-become-widows

[7] Wiser.org

3

IT WILL GET BETTER

"You can't stay in your corner of the forest waiting for others to come to you.
You have to go to them sometimes."
– A.A. Milne, Winnie-the-Pooh

Considering such unfortunate and unwanted events, I just want to tell you one thing: **It will get easier over time.** There is no proper way to cope with loss, and I won't attempt to prescribe a way to do so. A family therapist can tell you what steps to take next, but you have already taken a step by choosing to read this book. Every situation is different, of course. I recognize that there are commonalities in this area, but I also know we cannot compare them. Again, it is all right to cry your heart out, and grieve, but as you do, there are things that need to be attended to.

THIS IS BIG

Once you understand the difference between "fault" and "responsibility" you are genuinely ready to make major strides. Something has happened here, and it may not be one bit your fault. If you lost a relationship for any reason, that is not always the fault of the remaining spouse. If you lost a spouse to illness or accident, that is most certainly not your fault. But here is the lesson: ***While this moment is NOT your fault, it IS your responsibility to deal with it.***

When we take greater responsibility in our lives, we gain greater control. Here is an example of what I am saying. Here in Oklahoma, we have tornadoes. Those are NOT my fault. But it IS my responsibility to take action, to take cover when a tornado is in the area. It is so easy to assign fault in life, but it is VITAL that YOU take responsibility for taking the next steps. Remember, it's ok to rest, recover, and grieve. Rest is essential in the process. However, there will be a day when you've had enough rest, and you'll be ready to tackle these new responsibilities. Deep inside, you know you can do it. When you are ready, it is your responsibility to make yourself happy again. Time will pass by anyway, why not spend this time building a life by design?

The first step to recovery often begins with your friends and family. As we mentioned earlier, those you depend on for support during these times will eventually get back to their own lives. During these early days, make sure you rely on friends and family and allow them to support you. I've seen in many cases where the remaining spouse is worried about accepting help from friends, and I consider this one of the big mistakes. Your ego is not your amigo when it comes to accepting help and support.

Allow your support group to support you. Be willing to tell them exactly what you need. During a crisis, it's difficult for our friends to know how to support us. It's so easy to tell them, "Everything is fine," when in fact it isn't. One day down the road, these same people may call upon you for help, and I can assure you it is a gift to be able to give.

The second major step to recovery is taking the first step up the mountain where you begin to deal with the physical and personal aspects of change. There will be paperwork to do, accounts to change, passwords to change, and things to remove from your home. We will deal with these steps in Chapter 4. This chapter is about awareness and acknowledgement. Right now, things may be piling up, but in our next session, we will discuss the specific steps towards recovery:

WHAT TO DO NEXT

During Chapter 4, we begin to create a new goal plan for the next phase of your life. We will start the process with the mountain of paperwork you get to deal with. We will calculate your new Financial Vision. Remember that spiral notebook mentioned at the end of Chapter 1? You will want to have this for Chapter 4!

You may want to put on a pot of coffee at this point.

ENCOURAGING QUOTES FROM WINNIE THE POOH AND OTHER FAMOUS PEOPLE

"If you live to be a hundred, I want to live to be a hundred minus one day, so I never have to live without you."
— Joan Powers, Pooh's Little Instruction Book

"You can't stay in your corner of the forest waiting for others to come to you. You have to go to them sometimes."
— A.A. Milne, Winnie-the-Pooh

"Why did you do all this for me?' he asked. 'I don't deserve it. I've never done anything for you.' 'You have been my friend,' replied Charlotte. 'That in itself is a tremendous thing."
— E.B. White, Charlotte's Web

"Do I not destroy my enemies when I make them my friends?"
— Abraham Lincoln

"Growing apart doesn't change the fact that for a long time we grew side by side; our roots will always be tangled. I'm glad for that."
— Ally Condie, Matched

"Some people care too much. I think it's called love." — Winnie the Pooh

"How lucky I am to have something that makes saying goodbye so hard." — Winnie the Pooh

"I always get to where I'm going by walking away from where I have been."
— Winnie the Pooh

4
WHAT TO DO NEXT

"If you are depressed you are living in the past, if you are anxious you are
living in the future, if you are at peace, you are living in the present."
—Lao Tzu

Welcome to chapter 4. Things get a little more exact as we explore
your next action steps. Because your world has changed, so must
your passwords. Here, we identify several items that require your immediate
attention. While realizing you are grieving, also realize that these items can
leave you vulnerable if left unattended.

Let's grab your spiral notebook and begin the process of TCB: Takin' Care
of Business. (This could have been chapter 1, as a few of these things done
incorrectly can cause trouble.) Here is the **number 1** thing you should do if
you are in a divorce situation:

**Important Step #1: Change your passwords to all accounts, primarily
banking, savings, and investment accounts. Remove your former person
and delete all access to your personal items. This is equally valuable if you
lost your spouse to death. There are scoundrels in the world waiting to
take advantage. This is how we fight back!**

This can also include:

- Social Media Accounts
- Bank Accounts
- Investment Accounts
- Cell phone account
- Credit Cards
- eBay and social commerce platforms
- Life and Health Insurance accounts
- Anything with online access, including bill pay systems

Do not delay in this activity. It is vital for your safety and economic well-being to take this step. Remember, write down your passwords in a place where you can always find and edit them.

The following list contains a few of the things you can do quickly to build your life by design:

- Password changes
- Get a Social Security statement to determine your benefit level
- Change beneficiaries on life insurance, investment accounts, and retirement accounts
- Financial Forensics: Read your last six checking account statements to see what money is being electronically drafted from your account. There may be expenditures you aren't aware of. Maybe your former spouse was acquiring collectible items such as coins or stamps, and your checking account will provide the documentation for you. You may also find insurance policies and investment accounts when looking at your monthly checking account statement
- Remove former spouse from your cell phone plan, and make sure to change your password there as well
- Rewrite your will immediately to reflect your choices
- If you have debts, determine the exact amount of each debt on the day of divorce or death. Make a list of debts, account numbers, balances, and monthly payments. This will give you ammunition to get out of debt

This list is just a partial list of actions you can take. Whether it is divorce or death, these actions will protect you as you move forward. Imagine how you will feel when you have made it through this list! Yes, it can be difficult, but I can tell you that it WILL be worth it.

Below is an expanded Suddenly Single Checklist with which to begin your journey. I am always eager to watch even the smallest of accomplishments and how they turn into larger success stories.

SUDDENLY SINGLE CHECKLIST

- Change passwords on all accounts including investments, banking, insurance, cell phone, credit cards, or any other online bills.
- Social Security updates: start on www.socialsecurity.gov. You may want to do an in-person interview at a local SS office.
- Change names on bank accounts and investment accounts.
- Check all automated bank drafts for accuracy and necessity.
- Call cell phone company to remove unneeded lines. Change password to your account as well.
- Remove names from loans, debts, and accounts.
- Set up "Transfer on Death" for your personal and business checking accounts to reflect your preferred beneficiaries.
- Rewrite your will to reflect your current preferences.
- Analyze your current debts and determine a payback schedule.
- Do a health insurance update.
- Update the beneficiaries on your life insurance and change the password on the accounts.
- **Complete a full "_financial forensics_" on your checking accounts. You can look for unneeded auto drafts, insurance policies, investments, or anything that you need to be aware of. Any amount coming from your checking account or on your credit and debit cards should be evaluated immediately.**
- **Work with your financial professional to do an "Income Plan." Confirm you will have the right amount of income for your current and future needs.**

- Analyze all current investments and evaluate your risk tolerance.
- Estimate your current savings (non-investment grade) to make sure you have ample cash nearby.
- Sell or give away things you no longer need. You may have things of value, so it may be prudent to ask someone for help. This includes cars, coins, guns, collectibles, etc. Get rid of the extra car if you don't need it. Donate clothing.
- Create an "Asset Sheet" that documents everything you own of value.
- If you are a military widow, check with the VA for additional benefits that might be available for you.
- Check your bills and see what can be put on auto pay.
- Determine if you have pre-paid funeral arrangements.
- Confirm if your spouse is due any interests or assets as a beneficiary or trustee. Was your spouse someone else's beneficiary?
- Make a list of necessary home repairs and factor that into your budget.
- Determine if you should sell your home and downsize to something that is better for you. With your realtor or advisor, determine the value of your home and potential equity. Also, confirm the values of any other real estate or investment party you own or have an interest in.
- Confirm that your property tax and property insurance have been paid and are fully active on all properties.

So, these are things you will want to accomplish as soon as practical. As I have mentioned, changing passwords is the first and most significant step you can take. After that, the Suddenly Single Checklist will be one of your tools to move forward.

Important Step #2: Get a yellow highlighter. You will find it quite satisfying when you use your yellow highlighter to cross through this list as you document another great accomplishment!

That's right! Get a yellow highlighter and attack this list! You will feel so good as these yellow checkmarks begin to fill your list. We all need little accomplishments as we go through life. I've learned that BIG accomplishments are usually the combined value of lots of little accomplishments.

Let's take a moment and discuss a few of the things on the list that you may question:

First, is it really ok to get rid of all my spouse's clothes and possessions?

Mostly, yes. Don't do anything too quickly if you're uncomfortable. Ask your family, friends, or your church if there is anything they might like. Of course, wait until you're ready. You may even be most comfortable putting things in storage for a year or so. At some point, it will be time to make a decision. If you've given it enough time, thought, and prayer, you will do fine.

On a humorous note, if you are going through a divorce, it may be less advisable to give away your spouse's clothing and personal effects. It would be funny perhaps a few years down the road and to have a funny story to tell, but we are here to take positive steps.

My spouse is upset that I took them off our accounts, what should I do?

This is an area where I have seen much abuse happen and it is prudent to have a secure login for personal accounts. Consult with your attorney to make sure you are in accordance with the law.

Be Careful of Significant Changes Happening Too Soon.

During intense emotional turmoil, it's easy to make long term decisions to fend off short term emotional pain. "Retail therapy" is a real thing that gets those endorphins raging but can lead us down the wrong path. There's nothing wrong with spending money, but it's most prudent to wait on those bigger decisions. Should I change jobs, buy a new car or house, move to another state to be near family, or should I start a business?

There is no minimum waiting time for any of these. Be cautious when making BIG changes though. Sit down with a trusted friend or advisor and share your plans if that makes you more confident and comfortable. It is perfectly ok to delay making any major and permanent financial decisions when you are overwhelmed with emotion.

As you make these decisions, remember what God says in Psalm 46:10:

"BE STILL AND KNOW THAT I AM GOD!"

5
CHANGES

"All the art of living lies in a fine mingling of
letting go and holding on."
–Havelock Ellis

David Bowie wrote in his classic song, "Changes" that we must "*turn and face the strange*", which I suppose is much easier when you are worth $50 million dollars. Facing these strange new times is rarely easy and most likely outside the jurisdiction of a fabulous 3-minute pop song. I've often heard that "the only constant is change." In this section on change, we examine how to move forward through grief and how to begin the process of creating a new plan for your future.

When any relationship ends, the most challenging phase to get through is accepting that everything has changed. Things may never be the same, and the memories made together may slowly diminish. This isn't easy when you are accustomed to living life with your partner. There will be days when it will hurt the most, and you'll wish that everything could go back to what it was before. It can be a struggle to find the will to move on, even if you were the one who pushed for divorce. Slowly accepting your new reality is the key to a new chapter in your life.

I believe you will find value and comfort in understanding these stages of grief. Depending on your circumstances, you may have seen this change approaching for quite some time. Others may have been blindsided by this new challenge.

Examine these stages of grief and see if they apply to you.

THE FIVE STAGES OF GRIEF

In the late 1960s, a Swiss psychiatrist named Elizabeth Kübler-Ross made rounds in the news when she released her book, *Death and Dying*. In this book, Kübler-Ross attempted to create a model that outlined the way people grieve.[1] She accomplished this by working with terminally ill patients. This model was later known as the Kübler Ross Grief Cycle. It comprises five stages that a person may or may not experience during mourning. So, what are the five stages in the grief cycle?

DENIAL

The Kübler-Ross Cycle assumes that the grieving process of a person starts with **denial.** This is the stage when you don't fully acknowledge what has happened. Think of it as your brain trying to protect you from the uncompromising news. Your mind denies the new reality and refuses to believe anything can ever be the same again. You cling to a "preferred reality" rather than the "actual reality". An example of this would be when you receive news that you or someone you love has a terminal illness. The most common tendency is to deny that fact and think to yourself that the doctors made a mistake. You felt confused and afraid. Interestingly, the denial stage helps you cope up with the shock. It serves as a cushion to absorb the blow and prevent you from being overwhelmed.

ANGER

The second stage is filled with **anger.** This is when you question the fairness of life and look for other people to blame for the event. You may lash out at family members or your closest friends. If you're someone who has a strong faith, then you may also feel the itch of blaming God, asking where He was when you needed Him most. But here is what professionals have to say: let that anger out. It's a necessary part of the grieving process. It helps you heal faster from the pain of your new reality. Remember our section on fault and responsibility? Still, it is ok to grieve aloud. Suppressing your anger is not healthy at all. Do not be afraid to let it out - it will dissipate soon enough. Grief can leave you feeling isolated or abandoned. Those near you may be grieving also. The direction of anger toward something or somebody is what might bridge you back to reality and connect you to people again. Just be mindful of your words and actions - remember that they are grieving too.

BARGAIN

The third stage is all about making a **bargain.** It is, in some ways, a means to cling to false hopes. You may negotiate for a miracle. Despite the pleading, no amount of negotiation will bring back a loved one. You will start feeling guilty, and instead of blaming others, you blame yourself. You think that somehow, you're the one responsible for your grief, and you become stuck in endless thoughts of, "what if's." What if I drove home early that night? What if I did not ask him to come to pick me up at ten in the evening?

DEPRESSION

The toughest stage in the Kübler-Ross Cycle is **depression.** Depression and mental health are very real--it is not just an excuse to get a day off from the job. You may find someone smiling on the outside, but we'll never know how empty they feel on the inside. Depression is not just a way for people to ask for empathy. Depression does not always show outward symptoms. It represents the emptiness we feel when living, and realizing the person or situation is gone or over. In this stage, you might withdraw from life, feel numb, live in a fog, and not want to get out of bed. The world might seem too much and too overwhelming for you to face. This is the most complex and most crucial stage you must go through to heal fully. If you feel you are stuck, please find the motivation to talk to someone you trust. They can help you through these troublesome times.

ACCEPTANCE

Last, we have the **acceptance stage.** Similarly, to what I have repeatedly mentioned in this book, acceptance is the key to a new chapter in your life. George Orwell said it best, as I quote him, "Happiness can only exist in acceptance." This is where you will begin to re-enter reality slowly. You will gradually realize that your relationship with your spouse is over, or that they will never come back. It is a time of continuous change and re-change. After this period, you will get out of the fog, engage with friends again, and even form new relationships as time goes on. While there will never be a replacement for your loved one and all the memories you shared, you can move, grow, and change as your new reality progresses.

So those are the five stages of grief. However, please remember the Kübler-Ross Cycle is not linear - that means that you may experience other stages before the other. In addition, some people may or may not even experience them at all. While the Kübler-Ross Cycle cannot generalize how people mourn because of our innate differences, it remains a relevant guide to understanding how our behavior changes during emotional times.

<u>Thoughts on Recovery</u>:
Take the time to grieve. Whether it's divorce or death that has separated you, it's natural to mourn the life and lifestyle you lost. Things may not return to your "old normal," but taking time to reflect and evaluate are vital. There is no set amount of time to grieve a loss.

<u>RECOVERY BEGINS HERE</u>

There's a big difference in acting and reacting. Most of your response to becoming Suddenly Single is normal. We react to tough situations. It's normal to react to pain. In this section, we learn to take intentional steps towards something better. Reaction is involuntary. Action is on purpose.

<u>Keep a journal</u>. I've met numerous people who did this, and they showed improvements in mood and productivity. Researchers discovered in 2008 that people who chronicle their experiences in a journal are more likely to heal from traumas. Plus, a journal is an excellent way to look back and see the progress you've made. Journals are an effective tool for anyone looking to accomplish something new. As you cross certain milestones in your recovery, your journal will remind you how far you have come. Inch by inch, it's a cinch!

Enjoy company. Lean on your friends or someone you trust and seek emotional support. This can happen among friends and family, but there are many church groups and Meetup groups that offer emotional and well-being support. It's liberating to share with others who are enduring a similar situation. One of the best ways I've seen to begin a recovery period is to help someone else in their own recovery.

Reinvent yourself. Perhaps there's a moment you've imagined where you simply start over, a new canvas to paint the life of your dreams. Is this a new career? A new hairstyle, new friends, taking a moment to pursue your own passions for travel, charity, or finally getting around to writing that new book. During this down time, you might enjoy enhancing your education or starting a new business idea.

Make new friends. Friends are a true joy. Reconnecting with old friends has never been easier with social media platforms like Facebook and Instagram. As you move towards new waters in life and business, be intentional about the next group of friends you'd enjoy making. When we mature, it is much easier to recognize what we like and easier to find people with those same goals and passions. This is the first "easy risk" you may take as you begin on the recovery path. I've seen friends of mine who have reconnected with old family members, cousins, aunts, and grade school friends who somehow slipped away during life. Reach out. Say hi. I'm certain that old friends and family will be excited to hear from you. Make a good life for yourself with your friends.

As Winnie the Pooh says, "You can't stay in your corner of the forest waiting for others to come to you. You have to go to them sometimes."
A.A. Milne, Winnie-the-Pooh

Start dating again???? This is a tough one. Be cautious. One of the great mistakes I have seen after becoming Suddenly Single is a rush to the familiar. It can be challenging to be alone, regardless of the cause, but making another lifetime commitment too soon after leaving your previous lifetime commitment can be disastrous. When you are in the grieving process, everything looks vastly different. Love and companionship are different from one another. Make sure you're ready. In situations where a spouse has died after a lingering illness, I've seen it often that the grieving spouse marries a second time much quicker. My own stepfather, Bob, watched my mother die of cancer over a period of a few years. During this time, he and my mother discussed HIS future plans, and they had candid discussions about his plan to find companionship. Bob was remarried within six months after my mom passed. It was my mom's greatest wish that he finds someone to spend time with and to live life with. Now THAT is love!

Create a bucket list. This new life may also reopen old and introduce new interests. Is there a place you've always wanted to see, a book you want to write, or even a business you would like to start? Why not now? Other than basic survival, there are no rules when it comes to creating your next life. Investigate things that genuinely interest you. Is it possible you've forgotten what you truly value? Your bucket list can also be a great tool to make new friends who have the same interests as you do. Wouldn't it be nice if you reconnected with an old friend from college and took that 2-week trip to Italy that you've always dreamed about?

Have you considered being a volunteer or philanthropist? This could be a moment where you share your time and talents to help someone achieve their goals. Our church is always looking for volunteers in the Children's ministry. It doesn't take a great amount of money to be charitable towards others. Your time is valuable, and to be able to share it with others is truly a rewarding gift.

Get smart with finances. The biggest worry after becoming Suddenly Single is financial solvency. If you were in a relationship where someone else handled all the finances, this may be a great time to become the captain of your own financial ship. Classes and programs are plentiful and can be found online or in person. In addition, using a qualified financial advisor is a consideration as you chart your path. Seeking guidance from someone who has seen a situation like yours will be helpful. This is also a time to evaluate your financial plan. Will you have enough to retire, pay off debts, send kids to school, etc.? Using a qualified tax professional can also contribute to your success. Your tax burden has now changed, and it's vital to establish the right kind of plan tailored just for you. One thing a tax professional can advise you on is the RMD. If you are over 72, the IRS requires that you take "Required Minimum Distributions" from IRA and 401(k) type accounts. These are called "Qualified Accounts," and each year after the age of seventy-two, you're required to take these distributions by the end of the calendar year. If you fail to take your or your spouse's RMD, there can be penalties levied against you. Once again, touch down with a qualified tax person so they can advise you on your next action steps.

Get Help: You are not alone on this journey. There will always be people who will listen and help you get through tough times. For example, your close friends and family. Don't be afraid to talk about how you feel, o how challenging it is for you to cope with all the things happening around you. There's no shame in asking for help. Often, seeking help from a counselor is a good step. My wife and I have been married nearly 31 years and we still use the services of a professional marriage counselor who helps us soften the sharp edges of life.

Take Care of Your Physical Health. An interesting fact to know is that you are more likely to die within the first three months of losing a loved one. This isn't meant to frighten you. Instead, realize that your body and physical health weaken during the grieving process. You may lose your appetite or have trouble getting a night of good sleep. Grief can be both physically and emotionally exhausting. As hard as it may be to tell you to eat healthy or sleep well, I highly recommend that you prioritize your health and well-being. Self-Care is a trendy new word as we are just now realizing as a nation that it is our responsibility to take good care of ourselves.

Here are five things you can do that will change how you feel. These things are simple to do. However, things that are easy to do are also easy NOT to do. It takes a little discipline and continuity to get value from most things.

- **Drink half your body weight in ounces of water daily**. (Always check with a physician to confirm) Water helps eliminate toxins and will increase your step count on your Fit Bit as you spend a bit more time walking to the bathroom!

- **Take a nap**. Seriously. A good 20-minute snoozer is a game changer.
- **Go for a walk**. The distance doesn't matter at first. Just take a walk around the block. Take your kids with you, if they still live at home. Meet new people or just exercise with your dog.
- **Minimize carbohydrate intake**. I've found that carbs turn into fat. Consult a nutritionist, of course, and make sure you mention to your doctor what your new eating plan is like.
- **Journal**. I've mentioned it before, but it's worth mentioning again. Write down your thoughts, goals, and worries. This helps you leave your worry on the page and will give you a wonderful way to look back and see how far you've come. This way you can pat your own self on the back and say, "Way to Go"!!!

"THINGS THAT ARE EASY TO DO ARE ALSO EASY <u>NOT</u> TO DO. THUS, CREATING HABITS OF THESE THINGS IS UP TO YOU. YOU WILL BE GLAD YOU DID."

1 https://www.verywellmind.com/decisions-to-delay-if-youre-grieving-4065127

6
TAKING CARE OF THE KIDS

W hether death or divorce, your family matters during this time. This is another reminder that you aren't enduring this moment alone. Chapter 6 could be a book or seminar all on its own, so I will condense into as few words as possible. I've included some steps at the end of the chapter for your consideration. I pray that they'll bring you comfort and value.

<u>Minor Children</u>:

From a financial standpoint, minor children are treated differently than adult children, as they are entitled to certain benefits from Social Security, and "aid to dependent children". Make sure you apply for these benefits as early as possible after a death has occurred.

If divorce is involved, you and your attorney will negotiate the payments from your former spouse for child and/or spousal support.

However, the money is a small solution to a potentially bigger problem. First, I believe children are tough. From an early age, they learn how to endure, and problem solve on their own. I was one of those kids who was ripped apart by divorce, not once, but TWICE. My mom and dad divorced and remarried and divorced again. Seeing my protector leave our home was devastating for me.

As the surviving spouse, YOU are now THE ROCK of your family, and even though you are grieving, your kids need you more than ever right now. As tough as this is, it's ultimately a good thing as it gives you something to focus on. If they witness you crumble, that may add to an already tough situation. Keeping it together is challenging. Honestly, I have no idea how one could accomplish that. I am thankful I have not been tested on this myself, but I see it all the time. Mom or dad "steels up" for the benefit of the kid. This topic trends into a much deeper process of human emotions and grieving. I suggest you have a trusted counselor who can help you adapt to this new environment. It is healthy to talk about it and ask questions. Have deeper conversations with your children at every opportunity.

One of the things I have seen in a divorce situation is when one parent begins to speak poorly of the other spouse. I've seen parents attempt to get inside info on "**what was Mommy doing last Saturday night?**"

Life is beautiful. When two people create another life called a child, it's a miracle and worthy of praise. When these two people can no longer live happily together and have abandoned their vows, it devastates the child that one or both parents begin to attack and go on the offensive.

Look, if this is you, **STOP IT**. I understand that you're mad. I understand you're hurt and afraid. I've seen it up close in my own family. And while the child's life has taken a new path through no choice of their own, there is simply no reason to add to their devastation. One day everything is great, and the next thing you know, that parent whom they love deeply is being described as the devil.

Let me warn you: It will NEVER benefit you or the child to talk poorly of the former spouse. That former spouse is STILL 100% of the parent. There're always two sides of the story in every divorce, and your behavior can come back to haunt you later. Your kids will grow up one day. Give them a chance to still be children rather than mediators of an ugly divorce. You loved the other parent enough to marry and have children with them, and that implies a certain amount of respect on behalf of the children.

Remember Fault vs. Responsibility: the divorce may not have been your fault, but it is your responsibility to raise good citizens. Rather than placing the blame on the former spouse, place the responsibility on you and share that with your kids. Children ought not to be victims of the choices adults make for them.

That conversation might look like this:

"Kids, your mommy and daddy love you very much. You are our highest priority. Unfortunately, mommy and daddy aren't going to be able to live as a family anymore, but that doesn't mean we aren't a family. We love you with all of our hearts and will make sure you have everything you need as we move forward in this new environment."

FINANCIAL CONSIDERATIONS:

Make sure your will mentions your children as the primary beneficiary. Visit with an attorney about how to leave assets to a minor child, and how you might create some type of legal trust that could act as a beneficiary in case you die before they reach age 18. You can spell out how assets are to be divided and spent.

This part is tough, ugly and expensive, but it is necessary at some point. The last thing you want to do is leave your life insurance or retirement accounts to your former spouse and only assume the money will be spent in a way that you agree with. Take action.

There are other questions regarding helping kids plan for an education. If this is one of your goals, it is vital to visit with your advisor or CPA to create a funding plan. College continues to spiral in cost, so adequate planning is essential now.

Kids are durable. They can handle the truth. They can't handle a grown up attempting to verbally demolish the other parent. They can't handle not being able to visit freely with the other parent. It's up to you to provide the solution, which may be the hardest thing you've ever had to do. It's worth it.

Adult Kids: This one is more interesting. With adult kids, you can speak as an adult to another adult. Nothing you want to do requires their approval or consent. There's always a fine line between sharing with your kids the facts about your situation and asking them for advice. No one knows as well as you the internal workings of a marriage.

In the event of death, your kids can be your greatest benefactor. They are, of course, grieving too, but it was always my highest duty to take care of my mom when she was down. Grown kids are truly a blessing. Not just during chaos but in life. Be thankful you have accomplished something special. During these times, make sure to talk to your grown kids as often as possible.

SOME SOBERING STATISTICS

Here are some key statistics to help you better understand the profound impact of losing a parent to a child at this age.

On the death of one or both parents[2]

- About 40,000 children lost their parents to Covid-19.
- Almost 1.5 million children live at a lower standard of living because of a parent's death.
- Children who lose a parent during their formative years say that they miss the guidance their parents provided when they first became parents.
- 80% said that losing their parents was the most challenging thing they had to face.
- On average, it takes six years for a child who lost a parent during childhood to ultimately move forward.
- 57% say that support from family and close friends wane within three months.
- Almost 82% of children who lost their parent(s) have been observed to show withdrawal and less class participation.
- 68% of children whose parent (s) died were observed to have a decrease in the quality of their work.

On the divorce of their parents:

- Almost half of all children in the US will witness the end of their parents' marriage through divorce
- Children with divorced parents are more likely to experience injuries, asthma, and speech impediments.
- Children with divorced parents are 20% more likely to become less physically healthy.
- Adolescents living in single-parenthood, home, or blended families are 300% more likely to need professional psychological help.

- Children whose parents are divorced are twice as likely to attempt suicide as peers who have a traditionally complete family.
- Children from broken families receive lower grades.
- Children with divorced parents are more likely to develop psychological problems and risky behaviors (drugs, unsafe sex, etc.)

There are a lot of other physical, emotional, psychological, and emotional effects that a child can experience during and after the grieving process. It's also possible that the scars brought by a wounding event, such as losing a parent, won't completely heal. This can carry into their adulthood, negatively affecting how they build relationships or pursue their careers. As parents, it's our responsibility to help guide them in whatever way we can.

HELPING Children

It's normal to be unsure how to get started helping your child during the grieving process. If you're looking for a way to get started, here are a few tips I can share with you. You know your child better than anyone. This is simply a guide to help you navigate the complexities of dealing with such a tumultuous event.

Normalize grief. Be a solid figure for your children. Yes, you are grieving, but your responsibility as a parent does not stop when you lose your partner. I don't think it ever does. You've been their rock for as long as they can remember, don't change now. The way you grieve following the death of your spouse or divorce will affect how a child may process everything. There's no shame in showing emotions. Nothing is embarrassing about letting your snot run through your nose as you cry over your spouse's death. Make the grieving process normal. Remember that in their lives, your children will have to face something similar. Showing the kids that it's all right to grieve helps reduce the anxieties from losing a loved one.

It's no one's fault. Previously, we mentioned how the feelings of guilt often swallow us as we go through the grieving process. Children are no exception. Although less mature, they can also take on feelings of guilt. They may start blaming themselves for their parent's death, or even think that they're the reason you and your spouse filed for a divorce. Let them know that it's never their fault; the warmth and support you provide reduces anxieties and lowers the likelihood of negative psychosocial development.

Minimize negativities. If you continually highlight the loss of your spouse, your behavior will affect how children react to the event. Refrain from too much negativity. Losing a parent is difficult enough, so constant negative comments will not help with recovery.

Take it slow. It will take some time before the kids can eventually accept their new reality. There's no need to speed up the process. I've seen parents get stressed out and make unnecessary comments like, "He's not coming back, stop looking for him!" Also, some parents decide to date quickly afterwards. Your children have already been in shock, and it doesn't help if you feed them information all at once. Take it slow, grieving takes time.

Do not underestimate them. It's easy to think that they're just children and will always be. But the human mind is more capable than that. If their behavior can progress destructively without intervention, then there's no reason to believe that it can also be rewired to help them become better at coping with the stresses of life. Help them understand some events are simply beyond control and normalize the need to seek emotional support. Again, minimize the negativities.

Losing a parent is one of the most challenging things for a child. While we're in emotional turmoil following a divorce or death, keep in mind that the kids are in the same situation. You have been the pillar of support that they knew they could always lean on. There is no reason to change that now. Continue being the parent that they deserve and help them adjust. Your parenthood does not end at losing your spouse. It never does.

2 https://edition.cnn.com/2021/04/05/health/parental-deaths-covid-19-wellness/index.html

7

WHO GETS THE DOG?

"Every ending leads to a new beginning. Take what you've learned from your married life and use it to put together a new life."

Following a death or divorce, you may need to put everything aside to protect your interest. This may ensure that your financial future is in an excellent position. Keep in mind that your future includes long-term goals, such as comfortable retirement and financial security. By keeping all legal matters in check, you give yourself a better chance of being financially successful for years to come. Therefore, I recommended earlier that you change passwords to important accounts. The following steps are valuable for any situation you are facing. Taking inventory of assets and responsibilities occurs in both instances of death and divorce.

- **Prioritize the kids.** When recovering or preparing for death or divorce, extra considerations should be taken for the children involved. Discuss with your lawyer the options and scenarios that will include your children. This will consist of physical custody (where they will live), child support, legal custody, and visitation schedules (if applicable). Personal agreements such as where the kids will spend the holidays, or any special occasions should be considered.

- **Itemize your inventory.** A very crucial process in death or divorce is to have an inventory of all your tangible assets. Usually, this is done prior to divorce, where both you and your ex-spouse are required by the court to honestly declare all assets that you own. Try to make a list of all the personal items that you own, including heirlooms, jewelry, artworks, or even pictures that have some sentimental value. You should also create a list of all the properties that you jointly own with your spouse. Try to include as much of its value as possible and all the relevant paperwork. The list should include the real estates you own, vehicles, household items, and even pets. Remember that part of the divorce agreement is figuring who gets what. Put in writing who gets the dog.

- **List your non-physical assets.** Other than the tangible assets that you own, or jointly own, with your ex-spouse, you should also try to create a list of all your non-physical assets. These are assets that exist only in paper or other entitlements. Your list should include your 401 (k) plans, Individual Retirement Accounts (IRAs), bank accounts, credit cards, life insurance policies, and other policies that may include LTC plans, car insurance, disability, or health insurance. Be sure to include the account numbers and contact information for the companies that hold these non-physical assets. If possible, create both physical and digital copies of these assets, so you can easily access them when needed.[3]

- **List your liabilities.** Besides your assets, you should also create a separate list for all the debts you incur, whether on your own or with your ex-spouse. Your list should include your car loans, home equity lines of credit (HELOCs), mortgages, and any other forms of debt that you might owe. Like your list of non-physical assets, try to add the account numbers and the contact information of the debtors.

- **Collate legal documents.** To avoid the hassle or any future complications surrounding your divorce, it is important to keep together all the important paperwork and legal documents in one place. A simple binder will do the trick. This list may seem overwhelming at first but gathering them earlier helps you avoid the hassle of frantically searching for them later. Here is a list of the documents that you may have to compile.[4]

◊ **Marriage documents:** Prenuptial and post-nuptial agreements, marriage license, and divorce certificates.

◊ **Business documents:** receipts, business permits, trademarks, patents, and tax returns.

◊ **Tax returns:** federal and state tax returns for the past five years.

◊ End of life plans: Will, powers of attorney, healthcare directives.

◊ **Real estate:** Deeds, appraisals, mortgages, rental property records.

- **Update your beneficiaries.** This is the time to update the beneficiaries of your will. We mentioned in an earlier chapter that there are two major items you'll need to update outside of your will. One should note that updating the beneficiaries in your will does not ensure that your legacy is passed on according to your wishes. These two items require special attention:

#1 - Life insurance policies

Annuities and life insurance policies pass directly to your beneficiaries in most cases. Contact your life insurance company after a major life event such as a divorce, death in the family, or even remarriage to ensure that your intended beneficiaries are correctly listed.

#2 - Retirement Accounts

Like life insurance policies, both employer-sponsored plans (e.g., 401k & 403b) and individual retirement accounts (IRAs) will pass directly to your beneficiaries upon death. Reach out to your plan administrator to ensure that all the beneficiaries are updated and listed as you wish.

WILLS VS. TRUSTS

Many people confuse these two terminologies with one another, and the legal world can be confusing and expensive. Whatever your wishes are for the rest of your life, if you don't have it in writing, your wishes can be in jeopardy. If you don't have a will plan in place, your state authorities have their own plan in place. It is doubtful you would want to turn your assets or children over to the wishes of any government.

It is vital to get these items taken care of by a licensed attorney. Dying without a will is a complete disaster. In addition, you will want to discuss the addition of health care directives, powers of attorney, and directives to physicians. These are items that should be discussed with a qualified estate planning attorney in your area. When my mother passed away, we had properly executed final documents that allowed us to serve her best and final wishes.

"Your Will Is the LAST Love Letter You Get to Write to Your Family"

PROTECTING YOUR RETIREMENT

Without a doubt, retirement is one of the most critical phases of your life. It is a phase that, for years, has been among the number one concern for most financial professionals due to the changes of its landscape brought about by changes in government policies. Most Americans have more debt from credit cards than they have in their savings accounts. It's truly alarming when you realize that most of today's baby boomers might end up living poorer lives, during a time when they should enjoy the fruits of their labor.

PENSION SPLITS

Although the American style pension plan is a dying breed, many companies still have these types of accounts on the books and understanding your rights here is vital. Your pensions may be categorized as joint assets. That means that your pensions are subject to the division after your divorce. However, this process may vary depending on different state laws and rules on the division of your plan. Keep that in mind before making any big moves. Also, note that the division of your plan is not an automatic process.

Your spouse would need to file a document called a qualified domestic relations order (QDRO). The US Department of Labor defines QDRO as, "a decree that creates or at recognizes the existence of an 'alternate payee's right to receive all or a portion of the benefits payable regarding a participant under a retirement plan."[5] The spouse must complete this step before receiving financial contributions from your pension plan or retirement account.

KNOW YOUR BENEFITS

Before making any big decisions, you should also check the benefits included in your pension plan. It is important to have a core understanding of how your plan works to make a better decision when you divide the assets. For example, does the plan offer a survivor's benefit? If this was the case, then it's an option to maintain that benefit, instead of seeking a lump-sum distribution to be divided after divorce. That way, you can maximize the value of the pension plan. However, there will be some drawbacks, as this would be counted towards your annual income, which would increase the amount of income taxes you and your ex-spouse will have to pay. If you're unsure what is the best route to take when making these decisions, talking to a financial, legal, or tax advisor for additional insights might be helpful.

MAXIMIZING YOUR SOCIAL SECURITY

There are many factors when applying for certain Social Security benefits. During the onset of Covid, and the implementation of The Secure Act, many financial rules and regulations changed. It's important to seek counsel with your local Social Security office to determine which benefits you are eligible to apply for.

[3] Findlaw. "Checklist: Documents to Show Your Divorce Attorney." Accessed October 13, 2021

[4] Findlaw. "Checklist: Documents to Show Your Divorce Attorney." Accessed October 23, 2021

[5] https://www.dol.gov/sites/dolgov/files/EBSA/about-ebsa/our-activities/resourcecenter/faqs/qdro-overview.pdf

8
PLAN AHEAD

"Avoid the flying werewolf monkeys."
Dorothy

I would much rather be sitting with you over a nice cup of coffee talking about the weather, fishing, or my new dog. Unfortunately, that isn't possible at the moment, and it is time to dig in and make those plans that will carry us through the rest of our lives.

The best path begins with a simple estimation that *"I am right where I am at the moment!"* It doesn't imply you will be remarried. It doesn't imply you will start a new business and set the world on fire. It is a statement of status quo: As things are. At this moment, the only way through, is through.

We begin this section with some real-life advice on the hurdles you may encounter along the path. "Follow the yellow brick road" is wonderful advice, until flying monkeys fly out of the sky and begin to attack you. I am a huge fan of the Wizard of Oz. There are multiple life parables in that story, and the flying monkeys were always one of my favorite parts. In life, those unexpected things that can derail us and get us off track are predictable and avoidable, especially in our financial lives.

These obstacles, once known in advance, lessen the fear factor. I call those monkeys, "***The Four Dreaded Horsemen of Your Financial Future.***" These horsemen do not discriminate against your status - they affect everyone equally, whether they are rich or poor. You have heard the old saying – "*time is on your side.*" I disagree. Time is not on your side, at least when we break it down into its scary acronym:

- TAXES
- INFLATION
- MARKETS
- EMERGENCIES

THE T IN T.I.M.E. STANDS FOR TAXES.

Taxes are the first "Deadly Horseman" of your financial future. There are some interesting facts about taxes that I think you should understand. You will work from January 1st through May 1st just to pay your income taxes. Fifteen percent of every dollar that you have earned has been paid into the Social Security system. Do you count this as a tax? I do! Eighty-six percent of American taxpayers do their taxes wrong and overpay their taxes an average of $3000 per year. Eighty-six percent! Why would we ever pay a bill that isn't due? Finally, how big will the tax bill on your 401(k) or IRA be during retirement? There are multitudes of ways to get the tax planning wrong.

Consider this:

If you consider the overall nature of your financial life, I believe that taxes have been and will always be your single largest bill. How you choose to pre- pare your taxes is up to you. The Supreme Court has ruled that an individual has the right to arrange their taxes in such a way so as to pay as little tax as possible. It doesn't make you patriotic to overpay your taxes. Simply put, it makes you broke!

How then are we to deal with the touchy subject of taxes? People fear the IRS; they fear underpaying their taxes—which very few do. In my experience, the IRS is actually a quite pleasant group to work with. They're just out to collect what is owed, and not a penny more. If you ever have questions for the IRS, it's a great idea to include your CPA in those conversations, as they speak the IRS language. The biggest problems I see aren't ones inflicted upon our citizens. Nope! The biggest problems I see in the world of taxes are those problems that we volunteer, sign up for, and that we bring onto ourselves!

To top this all off, the Social Security payments that you receive during retirement may now also be subject to the federal income tax! Back in the 1930s when Social Security was introduced as "the old age savings plan," it was itself a tax on individual earnings. It was never meant to be taxed as income in any way. For millions of individuals and families who get Social Security, it is now included in the calculations for income on your annual tax return.

Unfortunately, *"tax reform"* brought new taxes on Social Security payments. Shocking! Does this bother you? I didn't think it was supposed to be this way. For 75% of the American population over sixty-five, Social Security supplies the majority of their retirement income. And for some, these payments may now be subject to the federal income tax. It is your responsibility to understand when and where taxes apply and what YOU can do to avoid them. As you rebuild your personal and financial life, taxes are those flying monkeys with fangs! Make sure you have your own plan to deal with these before they bite!

The I in T.I.M.E. stands for inflation. Inflation is the second Deadly Horseman of your financial plan. This is one of the true silent-but-deadly issues we deal with on an ongoing basis.

Simply put, prices are going up. In 2022 alone, the inflation rate is between 7-10% in different areas. Will your income keep up with the average price increases going on in the world? There are many kinds of inflation. The government reports the CPI, or The Consumer Price Index, as one measure of economic activity and inflation. Over extended periods of time, the government has reported that the overall inflation rate has been around 3- 4%. But I would ask you to consider what is called "personal inflation." Personal inflation is inflation on smaller, daily expenditure-type items, like milk, medicine, and gasoline. How much has the price of gasoline risen in the last couple of years? The price has almost tripled in some areas. How has your personal-inflation rate been affecting you?

Here's an interesting fact let's assume that inflation is 4% per year for the next eighteen years. What this really means to you is that over the next eighteen years the basic prices of things will double based on the inflation rate. To put this in better perspective, it would equally require that you double your income during the next eighteen years or learn to live on half of what you live on now! Think about that for a moment: learn to live on half.

MY DAD'S STORY

Growing up in a small town seems like an ideal life. In the early days, my father worked for the grocery store as a sack boy and managed to start his family on just a $200-a-month worth of income. And while things were very tight, somehow, we survived.

Sometime in the mid-sixties, my dad was offered a job with the Rock Island Railroad. This job, while much harder, also offered the availability of benefits, similar to a retirement-pension fund. It also came with a substantial wage increase, where my dad was making approximately $500 a month. Now when you're used to earning $200 a month, and you get a job making $500 a month, and it has a retirement pension to boot, it's easy to lure yourself to sleep thinking that you have it made.

Now if you could, just for a moment, put on your 1968 glasses and imagine going from $200 a month to earning $500 a month, and then have your employer promise you a lifetime pension of $1000 a month! That's right, a promise of $1000 a month once you reach age 65. To a previously poor family, the thought of making $1000 a month seemed wildly wonderful! Now, take off your 1968 glasses and imagine what my dad's life might be like in 2022 once his railroad retirement pension came to life. Someday is today, and it wasn't enough.

In this modern era with modest inflation, my father is now forced to live the rest of his life on just $1000 a month. What did the railroad pension forget to include? Inflation! That's right; a simple 3-4% inflation rate rendered what seemed to be an amazing retirement, unlivable just 40 years later.

My father was not a bad guy; in fact, he's a very good man. He is smart, articulate, and generous. But unfortunately, he was not prepared to deal with the negative impacts of inflation. They don't teach this in high school; they don't teach it in college, either! If you fail to learn and deal with inflation, you might get the same type of results. Consider how vast your own lifetime might be. Contemplate how long you will need your money to work diligently for you. Imagine what it might be like to retire at sixty-five, then live to age 100: you would have to live off your savings and retirement plan for thirty-five continuous years!

Inflation is a type of financial cancer, and it has very few symptoms. It just sneaks up on you, and before you know it, what once was a great retirement is now a paltry existence. Wealthy people understand and take precautions regarding inflation. How will you deal with this nefarious problem? The I in the acronym T.I.M.E. stands for inflation; the T stood for taxes. Both are flying monkeys of sorts.

The M in T.I.M.E. stands for markets. From 2016 through the end of 2021, we have seen unprecedented rises in the stock market. The speed at which the stock market operates can be scary, even for the savviest investor. Everyone has a different point of view on investing these days, but the one fundamental truth that seems to prevail is that people are afraid of losing money. As a licensed Investment Advisor Representative, it would be improper to give investment advice in this book. Before we advise on such subjects, there are questions to answer about your situation regarding time frames, income, and risk tolerance.

The market can be a joyful place and a fearful place at certain times. Coming through a death or divorce of a spouse adds additional levels of concern as you plan your future path. Numerous philosophies are out in the investment world, and as you work with your advisor on a new plan of action, making sure you understand your own risk tolerance is essential.

Here is another market risk to think about: what if your money is safely OUT of the market, and the market then shifts significantly upward? During the initial phases of the 2020 Pandemic, many investors took money out of the market due to fear, only to see the general markets accelerate by the end of the year. One risk is the market going up, and you aren't in it! Investing is still important if we are attempting to outpace the negative effects of inflation. In our current society, inflation is as high as it has been in many years. How might this affect your plan as you step forward to a full financial recovery after becoming Suddenly Single? These are the questions we must answer as you build your new road forward.

The general stock markets in 2008-2009 lost nearly 40%. What would that do to your economic future?

The E in T.I.M.E stands for emergencies. The last Deadly Horseman of your financial life is unplanned economic emergencies. What makes up an emergency? Indeed, the day-to-day frustrations of a flat tire or a broken refrigerator always hit us at an inconvenient time. Every emergency has a price tag with it. Later in life, these types of emergencies are less important than the bigger ones we might encounter. For this conversation, let's just have an agreement that somewhere in our life, we will have to shell out a few thousand dollars from our emergency fund for the day-to-day emergencies, and that we need to take better and more calculated steps to deal with the larger *life-changing emergencies.*

THESE EMERGENCIES CAN SHUT DOWN YOUR ECONOMIC ENGINE!

- **Disability.** If your income stopped today through no fault or choice of your own, how long could you live on your savings?
- **Medical Care.** Do you have sufficient reserves to meet deductibles, extended hospital stays, assisted-living requirements, or other medical emergencies? One in four people spend the last two years of their lives in some type of long-term care facility. If this happened to you or a loved one, how would this affect your financial life?
- **The unexpected death of a spouse or family member.** Are you prepared for the unthinkable? Would the loss of one of your Social Security checks set you back? Does your pension have spousal continuation benefits? Do you have ample "nearby cash reserves," or adequate insurance for these contingencies? Elderly parents for whom we take responsibility: with life expectancy increasing, what would it look like if you became the primary caregiver for an elderly parent or relative? Adult children with financial needs: Are your children independent of you? Have they somehow been your

economic priority? What is the right way to deal with your adult children?

- **Last-minute loss of job**. The cleanest of plans is no match for the mess of reality. Many of us have plans to work until a certain age, or we plan to exit the job market at a certain level of savings. What happens if your employer has a different idea than that? Are you prepared for the unexpected loss of fuel prior to crossing the finish line? With "pandemic" now being a common word in America, there are a variety of real things that can interrupt your lifestyle.

Talking about these things is just depressing, right? But it would be equally depressing to endure these things *without* having an economic plan to deal with them. Unfortunately, I'm not just talking theoretically. I see it with clients every day. Let's agree to discuss these potential emergencies, address them, then create and implement a plan to deal with the ravages of an unplanned financial life. You wouldn't get in your car for a long-distance trip without some kind of map. Let's make a few adjustments to your economic road map. Your economic engine will be fine with the right tune-up. You will too!

As we begin to build your new economic engine, here are a few things to consider. In my career, I have noticed some common behaviors that diminish the effectiveness of your plans. These are observations on my part from working with families just like yours.

THE MOST COMMON REASONS PEOPLE STRUGGLE TO ACCOMPLISH FINANCIAL GOALS:

- Buying and selling investments emotionally
- Procrastination and letting time slip through their fingers
- Panic—looking for the hot stock that will erase years of financial sin
- Having a short-term outlook on a long-term investment
- Buying investments because they are popular, usually after they've gone up in price
- Not understanding the tax ramifications of investing
- Becoming a "do-it-yourself" type person with products and services that normally require a license and take years to understand

- Bailing out your adult children and family members time after time, never letting them suffer their consequences. (*"Did Cash just say that? I am not sure if I like this guy!"*)
- There is no fool-proof formula to becoming financially stable. Even if there were, it would be an equation that minimized mistakes and maximized positive actions. Panic and crossing your fingers is a weak financial plan. As you recover from your recent loss, find the time to create and follow some type of plan.

Let's wrap this session up with a few thoughts:

T.I.M.E. = TAXES, INFLATION, MARKETS, EMERGENCIES

We have this tendency as people to blame ourselves more than necessary. The fact is, taxes, inflation, market issues, and emergencies are NOT your fault. You can take a breath here and recognize that life is tough sometimes. Here is the best lesson I learned as a young person when my own life was not turning out the way I had wished for: *"AT THE EXACT MOMENT YOU REALIZE THAT LIFE IS HARD, LIFE BECOMES EASY!"*

Some of you blame yourselves for the events listed in **T.I.M.E.**, and I want you to know that it isn't your **fault**. However, it is your **responsibility** to take steps from right here, right where you are. Give it all you can as long as you can. Winners run *THROUGH* the finish line, not TO the finish line. Accept the hard nature of life, and it becomes a beautiful, yet challenging, experiment!

9

STEPS TO A WINNING PLAN

"It takes as much energy to wish as it does to plan."
- Eleanor Roosevelt

Marriage is difficult. Two people that grew up in different households, lived in different environments, and had distinct personalities getting married to each other - you could imagine that inadvertently, there will be some road bumps that they'll have to overcome along the way. Marriage is also the most fulfilling part of our life! We imagine just how our marriage would be, from the time we were children, until that magical moment at the altar. And with the addition of children, a home, and a career, life can be quite fulfilling.

It isn't just marriages that suffer economic hardship. For the average single person, buying a new home, travel, finding the right kind of career, and saving for retirement can all be daunting tasks. Like most things of value, once a clear plan is in place, your chances of success may increase. A goal without a specific plan of action is simply a wish, and there's little magic in wishing for things to change. Change takes action, and YOU are an ACE.

FIVE STEPS TO A WINNING PLAN

It has often been stated, "You must become the change that you wish to see in this world." How often in your life have you wished that your situation would've turned out differently? Have you ever wondered what it would have been like to be born wealthy? What would it feel like for you to have a confident financial life as you grow older? The answer is simple. Have you ever thought about asking somebody how they went about accomplishing the very things that you would like to accomplish? Wouldn't it be great if somebody who was living the life that you'd like to live was willing to share their secrets of success? Consider it done!

For the past thirty years, I have worked with various individuals and families as they prepare, manage, and create their finances for the future. These clients have come in all shapes and sizes, from all backgrounds, and varying degrees of success. Over the three decades that I have helped people plan and prepare their financial lives, I have noticed a few common threads among these families. The steps we are about to discuss are common among financially successful people. To be successful, these five steps are fundamental habits. Habits make all the difference in our lives. First, we form our habits. Then, our habits create outcomes. Are there financial habits you would like to change? Are there financial things you would like to teach your children as well?

Coming from a small town, it was inevitable at some point, one of my relatives would also be one of my schoolteachers. In the third grade, my mother's distant cousin, Dorothy, was ill-advisedly assigned to be my homeroom teacher. Since I knew her as a family member, I suspected I might get by with a few more shenanigans than just the average student. During math assignments, I continually copied off Joe Mark Cowden, the smartest kid in the class. This guy was good, and I was a lazy third grader. It just made sense that I would copy his answers, since he had already gone to all the trouble to figure it out! It made no sense to me to reinvent the wheel. Aunt Dorothy had a vastly different perspective when she caught me "borrowing" other people's work. Because we were in a small town, she had an unrelenting fear of showing favoritism toward me, and more than doubled my punishment when she caught me cheating. Here is what I learned from that lesson: copying from somebody else who is successful is a high form of praise, but not at all legal in the third grade.

Cheating will get you five horrible swats from the principal, chalkboard cleaning duty, and a stern talking-to from a distant relative who seriously questioned whether I would be an okay citizen.

If you have successful people in your life who will share their tips with you, that is fantastic. In our culture, people often don't like to talk about money, religion, or politics. (Actually, the internet has changed our desire to talk about politics—it seems now everyone is a constitutional scholar online, as well as an epidemiologist.) These following five steps aren't things I read in a book, and they aren't items that you'll find somewhere on the internet. The formation and recognition of these five items, and the order in which they occur, took me three decades of observation to understand. You can learn these steps in a matter of hours. They work, and they work better if you use them in the right order. You wouldn't put the roof on a house until the walls were built, right? You wouldn't put the icing on the cake prior to baking it, right? (Silly example, I know...everyone eats the icing first!) What time and wisdom will teach you, if you are paying close attention, is a logical order in setting up your financial house.

Bonus Life Lesson: Cheating is bad; emulating positive and uplifting behavior is great! Knowing the difference is called wisdom.

Before you build a house, you would go through many preliminary steps to make sure the house plan was just like you wanted it. You would pick a neighborhood, a piece of land, hire your builder, review a floor plan, and solve other related issues first. Later, as the house is built, you would pick out a paint color, décor, and garage door openers. This is the logical order in building a house. So, what is the logical order for your financial house? Did YOU eat the icing before the cake was baked (new car, debt, etc.)? These are the steps that I've seen countless successful people use to win the financial game. Yes, it is okay to copy from their previously successful work. Aunt Dorothy would approve.

STEP 1: HAVE A CLEAR VISION OF WHAT YOU WANT

Imagine going to a restaurant without a menu. It would be chaotic. The menu answers the big question: what do you want? The more specific you are about your objectives, the more likely you are to accomplish them. You wouldn't take a trip without having a destination in mind, right? This financial trip you're on is the same way. You must assess your starting point accurately, and you must determine an ending point. That ending point could be your retirement date, the date by which you would like to have children, or the date you would like to build your dream home. The vision portion of your financial plan is not just about wants and desires. It also must include the speed bumps along the way—like inflation, taxes, or any other item that might interrupt your plan. Of course, this portion of your plan is extremely flexible. Do not be afraid to make changes along the way. You'll find that along the way, life will help you focus on what is truly important. Will it be children? A dream house renovation? What about leaving a legacy or creating an educational foundation? How might you best accomplish that from a financial standpoint? These are the questions that you should ask yourself as you begin your financial plan.

You have already been through some unplanned events recently, so it may make sense to fight back with a written strategy or road map to get you where you want to go.

The statistics in America are ominous. With eighty million baby boomers hurtling toward retirement without a plan, the need for good retirement planning has never been greater. A volatile market and inflation have left the wrong sort of dent in the universe for those over the age of sixty-five. Too many Americans are living below our country's poverty line after retirement. Some people are struggling financially when they can least afford it. These years, often referred to as the Golden Years, don't seem to have much gold in them. I think we could look at the current situation for much of America as the "Tarnished Years."

Those who avoided calamity usually had a plan in place. We have previously explored the plight of my dad, Charles, who went from being a sack boy at the grocery store to working for the Rock Island Railroad and retiring on $1,000 a month. In the past, a pay raise from $200 to $500 a month was astronomical. While his pay increased as he continued to work for the railroad, his Rock Island pension remained level to some extent. He is lucky to have a pension, given that Rock Island suffered terrible financial hardship. In 1965, if you told Charles he could retire on $1,000 a month in the future, that sounded great to a young father of three children. The problem here is that neither my father nor the Rock Island had a clear vision plan for the future. Simply put, they didn't understand or prepare for inflation. These are the type of speed bumps that must be included in your vision plan.

So how much money will you need during retirement? Again, it depends on what your goals and visions are. If you are looking to travel the world with a lavish lifestyle, then expect the price tag to be higher. Meanwhile, if you are looking to downsize and live a modest lifestyle, retirement may not be expensive.

Here is the catch: most Americans live paycheck to paycheck, and as a result, it is a challenge to keep aside anything for retirement or build an emergency fund that should cover at least three to six months of expenses, by a rule of thumb. In the United States, around 25% have no emergency fund at all, and only 23% have enough money to cover three weeks' worth of expenses.

With the retirement landscape today, it is crucial that you identify the lifestyle you desire and then assess what type of income it will take to enjoy the vision you have. Here is a simple mathematical equation to understand your number. We must make one assumption—that you are living on the right amount of money today and are at least surviving.

So, for a moment, imagine that I am your waiter at a fancy restaurant. I am surely going to ask for your dinner selections. Equate that to life…

- What do you want?
- Can you afford it?
- Who do you want on this journey with you?

Here is a quick inflation example. Let's say you are 50 years old and are living today on approximately $4,000 monthly gross pay. You would like to retire on an equivalent amount at age 68, including what Social Security might provide you. Let's assume that number is $2,000 monthly.

Using simple inflation math, and assuming inflation is 4 percent a year (today in 2022 it is MUCH higher), you will need to double your gross income in the next 18 years. What $4,000 buys today will require $8,000 to purchase that same amount of goods at your age 68.

After subtracting $2,000 monthly for Social Security, your monthly income need is now $6,000 monthly at age 68. Pretty simple really. So, how much will I need to accumulate in order to have that amount of money coming in for the rest of my life?

I use a concept called, "Economic Drawdown," which explains how much you can take annually from your investment account to achieve your monthly goals. You need $6,000 monthly, or $72,000 annually walking in the door every month to accomplish your goal. We then divide that number by the "drawdown percentage" to determine how large your nest egg needs to be.

Let's assume you decide to withdraw 5% monthly from your nest egg to fulfill your retirement goals. We then divide $72,000 (annual income needed) by 5% (withdrawal percentage), and it indicates that you will need to accumulate $1,440,000 to retire at age 68. Now we have a target to shoot for, and while it may seem lofty now, putting it off won't make it any easier to accomplish.

Of course, there are many factors when configuring your number. Make sure you work closely with your advisor or CPA as you work toward establishing a firm goal. Don't be discouraged by this number. Time is on your side for now, but it is important to get started. As we finish with the section on vision planning, keep the book of Proverbs in mind, as it states:

"Where there is no vision, the people perish."

There are many other things to consider in your vision plan, but retirement is what most people neglect yet worry about the most. Given that time and money are equally important, it is time, right now, to get started!

STEP 2: PREVENT IRREVERSIBLE MISTAKES.

In this chapter, we will learn how to protect ourselves and our families. We spoke of the Four Dreaded Horsemen of your financial life a few pages ago. In this chapter, we expand on some risks and how to mitigate them. Many of these risks are self-imposed behaviors, usually stemming from apathy or the false belief that there is no perceived importance of the item at hand. Let's dig a little deeper and see if any of these monsters are under your financial bed. First, let's define irreversible mistakes. An irreversible mistake is a mistake that can't be reversed. Plain and simple. Here are some mistakes that come to mind, all of which are preventable. Once you have decided to avoid these problems, worry diminishes, and you can move forward with much confidence.

Irreversible Mistake #1: Lack of a Properly Executed Will Package

This is not legal advice. This is life advice. They will package much more than just your ordinary will. It is all the items and documents that help make that part of your life bulletproof. For example, it is important to not only have your will set up but want to have a rock-solid plan in place. Visit with your attorney or estate planning attorney, and make sure each of these items is in place:

- Medical power of attorney
- Durable power of attorney
- Directive to physicians
- Advance medical directives
- Passwords and lock-box keys
- Custodial issues for minor children
- Special needs trust for special needs children

These are but a few of the things that you'll want to take care of with your legal team. Make sure you get all your legal questions answered by a licensed, competent attorney with whom you have a good rapport. It is also important to make sure each of these documents is updated as the situation warrants. You will want to keep a copy of this in your "Life Records Book," which is mentioned in a later chapter.

Irreversible Mistake #2: Not Buying the Right Amount of Life Insurance

Using the drawdown concept discussed earlier, it's prudent to own life insurance that would protect your family in the event of your premature death. There are many questions about life insurance we should answer. How much life insurance is enough? What is the right life insurance? How long do I need this insurance to cover my family and me? How have my needs changed since becoming Suddenly Single?

Consider this: A report by LIMRA showed that the average overall death payout from a life insurance policy in America was under $90,000. If your family received a check for $90,000, and you took a drawdown of 5% a year, how much would a $90,000 life insurance policy pay your family in the coming years? Answer: $4,500 per year (assuming a 5% drawdown). Is that what you wanted when you bought the insurance policy? It is important to buy the right amount, twenty times your annual salary, to make sure your family has enough money in the event of your premature death. Is your family protected?

Irreversible Mistake #3: Paying Off Your Mortgage Early

Homeownership is one of the greatest American dreams. For most people, a mortgage is a necessary tool required to own a home. Most families simply don't have enough money saved to pay cash for a house, and that may not be a good idea, anyway. Most mortgage loans today cost between 3.5% and 4.5%. Let's look at why people suggest paying off a mortgage early. Let's assume that you have a $225,000 mortgage on your house at an interest rate of 4%, and you're making payments over a 30-year (360 months) period. Your estimated mortgage payment would be $1074 per month. Should you take out your full mortgage term and pay all 360 payments, you would have paid $386,706 for your $225,000 home! That's $161,706 of mortgage interest paid over the life of the loan. Many people would look at this and proclaim it to be a bad thing. Rather than reacting to emotion, let's apply simple mathematics using some basic assumptions. First, what if we took the traditional advice and added $150 per month to our mortgage payment with the idea that we could pay our loan off early? These additional payments would indeed pay our mortgage off early. By paying an additional $150 per month, we would pay our mortgage off in 285 months, or 23.75 years. This would save us seventy-five payments of $1,074, for a total savings of $80,550!

This may look like substantial savings and almost seems inarguable that this would be the way to go. Once again, let's apply mathematics, not emotion, and answer this question: **what <u>ELSE</u> could we do with that $150 a month that might bring us similar or greater value?**

What if you could invest that **SAME $150 per month** ($1,800 annually for 23.75 years at 9% per year? (Disclaimer…9% is a fictional number and not guaranteed.) At the end of the same period, you *would have* accumulated $134,849 of *actual cash* in some type of savings or investment account that you control directly! At the end of 23.75 years, you would owe approximately $75,000 on your mortgage. You could take the cash you accumulated, pay the mortgage off, and have an additional $60,000 leftover. Yikes! The public perception, based on this mathematical example, is, to put it mildly, WRONG!

While one way looks preferable, the fact is, mathematics does not support paying your mortgage off early in this method that we call "inside the mortgage." Believing the contrary, we call paying it off "outside the mortgage." Mortgage money right now is cheap. It is also very tax deductible for most people. To pay off low-interest, tax-deductible money, with other monies that might earn a higher interest rate, makes no sense.

Irreversible Mistake #4: I Can't Even Say It-It's Too Egregious

Each year, my wife and I go through our budget, and look back at how we earned money and spent money. A few years back, I found a budget item that became a **"deep curiosity"** for me. I found out that my wife had been overpaying the electric bill every month for the last fifteen years! I couldn't believe it! Every single month for the previous fifteen years of our marriage, she had been sending our electric utility company an additional $250 per month! Wow! We had what I will call an "interesting conversation" that went something like this:

Husband: "Uh, why are you overpaying the electric bill $250 per month?"

Wife: "Because I'm afraid they will cut off electricity, and I don't want to be left in the dark!"

Husband: "I'm sorry, I still don't understand. Explain it to me some more."

Wife: "It isn't that big of a deal. Every April, they send me a full refund of the overpayments, so it's sort of like a savings account for us."

Husband: "Savings account? Does it pay an interest rate? Do we have access to it during the year?"

Wife: "Not really. But at least we know we get to keep the electricity turned on. And by the way, if you want to take overpaying the bills, you may jump in if you see fit."

Husband: "I'm seeing it your way, sweetheart!"

This conversation never really happened about the electric bill. But I think you'd be shocked to find out that this conversation happens in 86% of all the tax-paying homes in the USA. We're not talking about the electric bill at all, we're talking about your income taxes. I believe one of the craziest things a family can do is to overpay their income taxes regularly. Why would you ever overpay a bill that simply is not due? It doesn't make you more patriotic. It doesn't make you less likely to be audited. It just makes you more broke!

This is an irreversible mistake if done throughout a lifetime. The average tax refund in North America is around $3,000 per year, and 86% of taxpayers get these types of refunds. Is it any wonder that our population struggles financially? This type of behavior must be stopped immediately and at all costs. If you are a voluntary bill over-payer... Stop it!

- You lose the purchasing value of your money
- Your cash flow goes down
- You could pay off other things or save for the future
- Your money earns zero interest

Waiting around for your money to show back up is the worst form of money management. If you don't know how to deal with your income taxes properly, seek the help of a professional tax advisor. These behaviors linger in families for years, and the compound effect can devastate the outcome of your financial life.

Again, ***IT IS NOT HOW MUCH WE MAKE; IT IS HOW MUCH WE KEEP!*** And if you keep sending extra money to the IRS for no apparent reason, you alone have made your financial road more difficult.

STEP 3: SAVE A LARGE GOB OF CASH

Step number 3, save a large <u>gob</u> of cash, is not that exciting. It is self-explanatory. And from the outside, this may seem like plain-vanilla advice. In a world of complex ideas, having an emergency fund ready for the unexpected, though very simple, is one of the single most important components of a well-orchestrated financial plan. Oh, and plain vanilla is still the number one selling ice cream in the world!

Take a moment right now and think back on the emergencies you have encountered in your life. Flat tire, broken refrigerator, loss of a job, illness, and the list goes on and on and on. Might there be other emergencies in your future? The primary reason that good families end up in **BAD DEBT** is that Step 3, Save a Large Gob of Cash, **has been skipped or forgotten.** Don't ignore this step. It is VITAL to your well-being and peace of mind to have the right reserves. Taking care of this step will make you feel better and be better prepared for the road to come. How much is enough? Like most answers, it depends. For some, two-three months of the reserve is enough. Others are more comfortable with more. There are multiple ways to accumulate cash. Here we illustrate a few budgeting and cash-accumulation ideas that might help you get started:

- Stop getting a tax refund and put those dollars into your monthly budget
- Save a dollar a day starting today
- Save your change every day, but put these dollars into a long-term savings account each year
- Borrow from your 401(k) to pay off higher-interest rate debts, credit cards, or obligations
- Limit your 401(k) contribution to exactly the amount matched by your employer
- Seek the wisdom of prudent people: check out websites, listen to podcasts or do your research.
- Drink water while out to dinner; then go home and deposit the exact amount you might have spent on drinks into some type of savings account

- Remove unnecessary subscription bills. If you're not a particular TV fan, then cutting off your Netflix subscription might be a good move.
- Go through your bank statements, and find auto-draft items that you no longer use or enjoy; cancel those unused health club memberships, pet insurance programs, travel clubs, etc.
- Refinance your house to a lower interest rate, and an extended term if possible; consider using these funds to pay off debts; use a competent, licensed, mortgage advisor to discuss options.
- Seek advice from a competent, licensed insurance professional about adjusting deductibles and other items on your various insurance plans.

STEP 4: INVEST FOR THE FUTURE.

Finally, we get to the fun stuff! Here we offer those bits of information that make guys like me the life of any cocktail party. (I've never actually been invited to a cocktail party, but should that trend reverse, I will proudly share this information.) The negative impact of inflation is eroding our purchasing power. What costs one dollar today will cost two dollars shortly down the road. It's harsh that we may spend as much time during the retirement years, (also called the decumulation, or income phase) as we did in the earning years. Because of the increased longevity of people, the retirement equation and the investment equation must be addressed adequately. We invest during the accumulation phase. We spend those investments during the decumulation, or income phase.

Therefore, the rules of how our investments work may be radically different during the decumulation phase than they are in the accumulation phase. Downward market swings might be to our benefit during the accumulation phase, as we continually contribute money into our accounts. But, during the decumulation phase, we are no longer contributing new dollars towards our retirement. During this time, we're only taking money out of our retirement plan. The rules of each phase require different strategies.

THE BASICS OF INVESTING

After working with clients from all walks of life, I have summarized the basics of investing successfully in the four basic areas:

- **Get started!** There is nothing more important than the act of starting.
- **Put your money in a good spot.** You don't need a bunch of crazy ideas designed to double your money overnight; you don't need to add a bunch of risks. Be reasonable! Meet with a licensed professional to discuss your options.
- **Watch over it.** Have meaningful conversations with your advisor. Ask lots of questions. Be involved in the process to a reasonable degree. At a minimum, have an annual checkup with your money just like you would your health.
- **Understand taxes and fees on your investments**. Not only can the market play a negative role in your investments, so will taxes. Make sure you understand your obligations tax-wise as you build your investment portfolio. The market will have periods of appreciation and depreciation, but the money given back to the tax system will never return to your portfolio.

INVESTING OVERVIEW

In this process, you are learning the five clues to a solid financial plan. Investing is clue number four, and there's a reason it is in this order. The dollars saved in your emergency fund are just as important as the dollars saved in your investment portfolio. Why? Because when you have an emergency, **you don't want to pull dollars for a short-term emergency from a long-term investment account**. That makes sense, right? Investments are long-term, and emergencies are usually short-term. Doing these things out of order could wreck your financial plan.

Let's summarize the first four steps that we have learned in this chapter:

Step 1: We need a clear vision of what we want. When we go to a restaurant, we order from the menu. You would never go and just say, **"bring me food."** Seeing is simply deciding what you would like for dinner, finding the recipe, putting the ingredients together, and then enjoying the delicious meal you have made.

Step 2: We must prevent terrible mistakes before they happen. This is the yucky stuff that we have to get past to avoid having to talk about it again! Nobody enjoys talking about death, disability, or taxes. So, wouldn't it be better to deal with it once on the front end? Once we have acknowledged and dealt with these potential risks and taken the right action, you will be better prepared when something unforeseen happens.

Step 3: We must save a large gob of cash. Step three, done correctly, will assist us in steps four and five. You don't want to raid your investment account every time a car tire goes flat. The biggest reason we go into so much debt is that somewhere along the line, we skipped step three. Don't skip step three. It is vital!

Step 4: We must create a reasonable investment plan. This is something long-term in nature, built on a reasonable understanding of our risk tolerance and not a put-and-take account. It is also in alignment with our tax objectives.

Let's introduce the fifth and final concept of the Five Steps to developing a strong financial plan. This concept is ***G.O.O.D.***!

STEP 5: GET OUT OF DEBT

Rule: The borrower is a slave to the lender.

First, let's establish a definition of good debt versus bad debt.

- Good debt = tax-deductible, low-interest mortgage debt. Certain low interest temporary loans.
- Bad debt = everything else.

Sometimes a low interest, defined term car loan will be to your advantage. Having lots of payments, however, can add stress to your plan. If you have accumulated cash, and begun a meaningful investment program, you might wonder why you should invest prior to getting out of debt. That's a significant question, and I'd like to answer it directly. Other financial authors believe you should get out of debt at all costs, and as early as possible, and I don't disagree with that. But I believe that missing a year of investing today has such an enormous negative impact later in life, that it just makes sense to establish a good habit now (saving) to replace a bad habit (debt). The cost of waiting to invest is simply too high to put off for another year.

Also, the reason most people choose debt is BECAUSE THEY SKIPPED STEP 3. Once you eliminate the primary cause of debt, your chances of staying out of debt are better. Saving money is a habit. Habits help you make progress. Bad habits (spending everything you earn) create more problems. Like I mentioned before, prioritize what makes sense. Does it make sense to put money in an investment that gives you a hypothetical return of 8% annually, or pay off a debt that charges you 4%? I hope that by now, this is clear for you.

Once you complete these five steps, you now have the power to change your financial life forever! If you have made it this far, I want you to know, sincerely, that the author of this book is very proud of you! Doing crazy things like overpaying your taxes does not make you more patriotic. However, living a prudent and thoughtful financial life is one of the most patriotic things you can do. Weak families elect weak leaders. We need financially solid families, and we need them right now. It is your obligation to lift yourself, dust yourself off, and move forward towards a better life that you have designed (Fault and Responsibility). Don't cop out and wait for any other human to do this for you. This is on you. Yes, YOU! Your current Suddenly Single situation has been your shadow for a bit...this is where we disengage from that set of problems.

Remember, it is the slight edge that will make all the difference for you. Little things add up to a lot of things. Gaining two extra pounds a year from high school to the age of fifty is a catastrophe. Saving $25 a week since high school can give you the slight edge in your finances. Ignoring the compound effects of a little money saved over a long period at a reasonable interest rate is an equal catastrophe. At the end of your economic life, you'll find your tummy to be fat and your wallet to be skinny. To pay your bills, pay for your lifestyle, pay for retirement, and pay for your dreams, you must first have the ability and willingness to pay attention to the little things!

You didn't come this far just to come this far. These items of discussion may help you surge forward in your goal set both financially and emotionally. We're getting close to the end.

FINISH THE RACE.

10

MONEY IN MOTION - INVESTING IN THE NEW ERA

"It takes twenty years to build a reputation and five minutes to ruin it. If you think about that, you'll do things differently."
-- Warren Buffett

Rule: ROI Should Stand for Reliability of Income, NOT Return on Investment!

Let's take a trip back in time to 1980:
- "Pardon me; do you have any Grey Poupon?"
- "Who shot JR?"
  - ◊ Fans of CBS's *Dallas* television series
- "Here's Johnny!"
  - ◊ Jack Nicholson, in *The Shining*
- "No, I am your father" (NOT Luke, I am your father)
  - ◊ Darth Vader, to a surprised Luke Skywalker

Mount Saint Helens was exploding. The stock market was about to explode similarly. The brilliant questions of the day were, "Who shot JR?" and, "Pardon me, do you have any Grey Poupon?" The first computer modem was invented. The Post-it note went live. The beginning of a new era in investing was upon us.

Employers were beginning the shift from defined benefit plans, pensions, and the creation of defined contribution plans (IRA, 401(k)). The Dow Jones Industrial Average was 759 compared to 35,000 as of this writing. A benefits counselor named Ted Banna was deciphering the tax code in 1980 and helped create the first 401(k) plan. Things were about to change in a big way.

During this time, public access to the stock market was limited. Many of the firms that existed were purely for the benefit of the wealthy and didn't have a high service level for the middle class. The fact was few people had a broker or an advisor during the late 1970s and early 1980s. Creating the 401 (k), the IRA, and the pending accessibility of market instruments through the internet was about to create the perfect wave of market acceptance of individual long-term investing. A cultural shift was taking place, and nobody could stop it.

Fast forward to today in 2022, most working Americans has access to the stock market. Instead of just a handful of people, everybody has the availability to buy stocks, bonds, mutual funds, IRAs, Roth IRAs, or can take part in a 401(k) through an employer-sponsored plan at work. The fact is the market is now available to everybody. On a more interesting note, eighty million baby boomers are speeding up toward retirement at this exact moment. Nearly 10,000 people a day will turn sixty-five for the next twenty-two years. In the stock market, the retirement planning market, and the personal finance world, we're witnessing the first measurable round of results from the switchover in thinking from company-sponsored plans to individually funded plans. Round one of the investing wars is over.

Take a moment now, look back, and contemplate how well your investment accounts performed. In this section, we will introduce three unique viewpoints on investment concepts. We will not be discussing any specific investment, any specific insurance company, or any specific annuity product. Instead, we will look at each of these areas generically, that we might leave this chapter with a broad understanding of other alternatives.

HOW DOES IT ALL WORK TOGETHER?

The money-in-motion flowchart (p. 70) shows how a typical family might orchestrate their money from the moment they earn it to when they invest it. The starting point for the Money-in-Motion Flowchart is money earned (Circle

A). This is usually as wages for most people. These dollars flow into your checkbook, which is shown by the arrow to the right. Circle B allocates actual cash, whether you keep it at home, in your wallet or purse, or a coffee can, buried in the backyard. It is vital to always have immediate cash. Of course, the amount can vary, but you will find yourself in situations where your Visa card is no good, and you simply need a stack of money to remedy the situation. Circle C is the reserve account we talked about, or your emergency fund. We also call this a "float account." For example, let's assume that you are most comfortable keeping $10,000 in your float account. You have also decided that should this account go below $7,000, (your trigger amount) you would make certain allocations and changes to fill it back up to the original $10,000.

Once you earn some money, put some money in your checkbook, stash petty cash, and create a float account, this is the perfect time to speed up your investment contributions. The four circles below your reserve account represent varying types of investments that you might choose to hold your long-term investments.

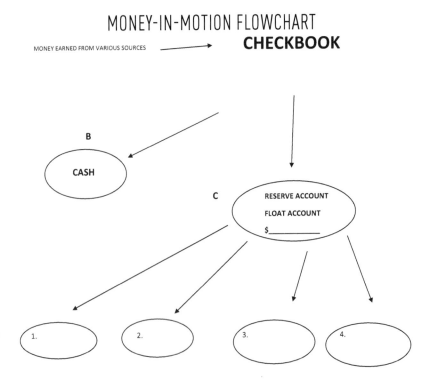

MONEY-IN-MOTION FLOWCHART

BASIC RULES OF INVESTING

Purpose: The dollars that you are investing are for the long term. There should be little or no consideration of using these resources anytime during the next five years. In addition to the Basics of Investing mentioned in Chapter 9, these rules will guide you as you develop your own personal investment plan.

- Your investment dollars are not for emergencies; these dollars are not to buy a house with; these are long-term dollars.
- You should know, and be comfortable with, the risk of each investment. You need to have a keen understanding of the potential downside, understand the program's fees, costs, and limitations, and understand the potential upside limits.
- Work on becoming bad-debt-free.
- Have a basic understanding of how each of your investments will be taxed during the accumulation or decumulation phase.

The rapid evolution of the financial system has made some of the past investment strategies practically obsolete. Long gone are the days when you can just simply let your money sit in a cash deposit account and earn 7% risk-free. Now more than ever, you need a solid investment strategy that allows you to maximize your returns and minimize the risks. As economic policies continue to reshape the landscape, you should also adjust your strategies appropriately. Stay ahead of your goal through mindful investing. Talk to your financial advisor and ask meaningful questions. It's always better to be informed about these matters before making any huge decision.

GPS BACK HOME: NOW WHAT? (PART 2)

With everything going on in your life right now, financial information and opinions can seem overwhelming. While I understand that many emotions are involved, I also know that moving on may not be the easiest thing to do. You might still be confused or unsure of the next "right step" to take. That is understandable. I believe Action Cures Everything. A.C.E. There will be some actions here you take easily and confidently, and some that require a bit more time. I get that and respect it. One of our goals is simply to wear out your yellow highlighter as soon as possible. Tackle that list as soon as possible, and your confidence will begin to grow.

Financial independence is difficult to achieve, especially during times of sorrow and grief. Making money can also be complicated during this season of life. Being Suddenly Single creates this recognition that everything is now on your strong shoulders. The reality is, now you can create a team of people who share some of the burden. You're now more equipped and prepared to take the next step, as soon as you're ready. Put on your best coat and get started today! You don't need to rush, just get started, and do something every single day.

While it DOES take consistent effort, you also need to take care of yourself. Take days off, spend time with family and friends, where recovery and money are NOT the primary topic of conversation. A vacation is in order: beach time is wonderfully medicinal! If you are reading this right now, I would like to thank you for sticking to the end. It took effort and time to put this book together, so it would mean the world to me if at least one person was affected by what I wrote. You are now one step closer to making your retirement and success dreams come true, and for that, I'd like to congratulate you.

As we come to a close, I hope that this book, ***Suddenly Single***, has provided some comfort and confidence as you move forward. Losing a loved one is tough. Those uncertainties will diminish, the lights will get a little brighter, and you can move forward gracefully. God tells us in the book of James to ***"consider it pure joy when you face trials..."*** I know that can be a challenge. Right now, you're becoming stronger with each day. You have already made progress. You can rest, knowing that you're prepared now that you're taking steps...you AND your yellow highlighter.

Contact the author:
cash@solomonway.com

Web: www.solomonway.com

Linked In: http://linkedin.com/in/cash-matthews-0778a93

Facebook: Suddenly Single: https://www.facebook.com/Suddenly-Single-2168640983150687

<u>Financial Disclaimer:</u>
In certain parts of this book, we illustrate certain investment rates of return that are NOT guaranteed or estimated. These interest rates are hypothetical and subject to being completely wrong. You must carefully examine the investments you use and determine their efficacy in achieving your results. No particular investments are mentioned in this book. <u>PLEASE DO NOT USE THESE NUMBERS TO CREATE YOUR PLAN</u> unless you have carefully studied the investment markets. No guarantees or outcomes are predicted or suggested in this book. Past investment performance does not predict future results.

Investment advisory services offered through Wealth Watch Advisors, an SEC registered investment advisor. Wealth Watch Advisors and The Solomon Group are independent of one another. Please note, registration with the SEC does not denote a specific skill level or guarantee the success of a particular investment strategy.

ABOUT THE AUTHOR
CASH MATTHEWS

Obviously, I am writing this about myself, which is a completely odd thing to do. So, I am 6'2", very muscley, a great humanitarian, kind, humble, and I love children and puppies. Did I mention humble? Ok, enough of this weirdness. I didn't graduate Aunt Dorothy's third grade regime just to stop there. There's more to the story (I am 5'8", by the way).

Yes, my name really is Cash. My dad named his two boys Cash and Carey. I'm in the financial world, and my brother carries people. He's a pilot. Dad worked at Thurman's Cash and Carry grocery store in our hometown and thought naming us this way was hilarious. Good one, dad.

When I was 8, I firmly told my mom I would never get a real job. I could hunt, and fish, and cook, and never minded sleeping outside. It's awesome at age 8 to be an underachiever. At age 14 I interviewed the smartest, richest man I knew. I asked him how he got rich, and later that day he introduced me to the market. He connected me with his broker and helped me set up a "custodial account" where I could buy and sell stocks. That's where it began.

I finished High School at Shawnee, High School in Oklahoma, and graduated from Central Oklahoma State University with a Business Degree. My graduation from kindergarten seemed more meaningful, however.

I started working in the financial business very quickly and have been doing just one thing now since the early 1980's. My office phone began to ring with similar sounding people who were suffering a divorce or a death. This idea of Suddenly Single simply showed up at my office. I witnessed it for years. Finally, I knew I needed to write about it. This is the result of being nearby for so many divorces, that I can't count them all. I've watched families suffer this strange fate called death. From a financial and recovery point, we need to talk about it.

I grew up in Oklahoma but headed to Texas in my late 20's. I was glad I was open when God shared a vision of me living in Tulsa, a place I hadn't visited much. My wife, Katy, and I have two children, one of whom is 13. I am 60. She is just like me yet speaks an alien language. ***The other is 22 and also the favorite. Like so super the favorite. 110%. She also isn't writing this currently as my editor. Nope. Just me. Cash Matthews. Business Boy Extraordinaire.***

Oh yeah, I was a BMX rider. I get Googled a bunch, and people inevitably say to me, "Hey, I looked you up on the internet and saw a guy 15 feet in the air on a BMX bike. That can't be you". Well, it is me. I love bicycles, and fishing, and golf, and writing, and puppies, and my family, and food. Only one of those endeavors landed me in a sports Hall of Fame. I was inducted into the National BMX Hall of Fame in 2006 and have served on their board since that time. Not a lot of BMX guys on Wall Street. Not a lot of Wall Street guys at the BMX track. I get it, I am a little odd.

What you are going through, I've been through with many families. I would be honored to stand with you as you take the right next steps. You and your yellow highlighter.

HUMBLE BRAG SECTION:
AUTHOR:

- The Solomon Way, 2015
- Money University, 2016
- Financial Meatloaf 2018 (This one cracks me up because the Wall Street guys with snappy red ties and clear polish on their nails don't understand how to find humor in what we do.)

- How I Lost 50 Pounds on the Keto Diet, 2020
- Suddenly Single, 2022

BUSINESS AND OTHER THINGS:

- Created Vacation Business School (VBS) to teach kids about God's plan for money, 2012
- Developed Business Owners Networking Group, Austin, Texas into a 3,700-member networking club. Unfortunately, the acronym spells BONG, and I found out that is a drug thing. I created the Austin BONG and the Tulsa BONG, 2009-Present.
- National Forensic League, Double Ruby Award, 1979
- Harvard National Debate Symposium, Top Speaker, 1979

Made in the USA
Middletown, DE
11 May 2022

65619314R00044